ASTON MARTIN
VANTAGE N24
V12 VANTAGE S

13-ISBN 978-0-9576664-3-6

www.cppress.co

First published 2015

CP Press. Hockley, Essex, SS5 4QY. England.

Acknowledgements

We wish to extend our sincere thanks to Grange of Brentwood for their help in compiling this publication. Thanks also to Richard Stewart Williams, Desmond Smail, Nicholas Mee and their Companies. Additional thanks to Tim Cottingham of the Aston Martin Heritage Trust.

Other Aston Martin Titles from CP Press

Aston Martin DBS, DBS V8, AM V8, PoW

Aston Martin DB7, DB9, DBS

Aston Martin Zagato

Contents

Aston Martin The Key Players 6

The Homes of Aston Martin 31

Aston Martin Vantage Race Car 36

Aston Martin V8 Vantage 38

Prodrive Rally GT Vantage 49

Aston Martin Vantage 50

Aston Martin Vantage Convertible 52

Aston Martin Vantage N24 54

Aston Martin Vantage DBR9 59

Aston Martin V8 Vantage S 75

Aston Martin V12 Vantage S 79

Lionel Martin

Lionel Walker Birch Martin was born on 15th March 1878 and was the son of E.M. Martin and his wife.

Robert Bamford and Lionel Martin joined forces to run a motor business in Callow Street, Fulham Road in 1913. They bought and sold small cars of the time such as G.W.K., Calthorpe and Singer. The firm did not stay at Callow Street very long for Hesse & Savory allowed them to take over premises at Henniker Place, South Kensington. Jack Addis was to join them as Works Foreman at Henniker Place while Robert Bamford was Manager.

In competitions of the day Lionel Martin had many successes with a modified and tuned Singer. This led to requests from customers for similar modifications to their cars.

The First World War saw Lionel Martin selling off all the machinery at Henniker Place, South Kensington to the Sopwith Aviation Company in Kingston, Surrey.

The first priority after the war was to get back together all those who had formed Bamford & Martin Ltd. Before the war and in January 1920 they moved from Henniker Place, South Kensington to 53 Abingdon Road, Kensington. The first prototype was registered AM4656 and was described in The Motor in November 1919.

Lionel Martin, his second wife Katherine and their young son John moved to "The Hollies", 1 Pembroke Villas, Kensington to be nearer to the Abingdon Road works of Bamford & Martin Ltd. Lionel Martin had always appreciated that in order to sell his new products he had to bring the name of Aston Martin to the forefront of the competition events, particularly those such as Brooklands. Lionel Martin's 'final' prototype (AM270) won the Essex Short Handicap at Brooklands in May 1921 with himself driving. In the Le Mans of September 1921 B.S. Marchall gained sixth place in his Aston Martin, "Bunny". Others who competed with Aston Martin cars included Victor Bruce who drove "Coal Scuttle" and Kensington Moir and Count 'Lou' Zborowski.

In 1924 Aston Martin saw 26 cars leaving the Kensington works for customers while new additional Aston Martin drivers for 1924 included H.S. Eaton and Victor Gillow.

**Henniker Mews was where Bamford & Martin Ltd started, moving to 53
Abingdon Road in January 1920.**

Lionel Martin, his wife and young John moved to 'The Hollies',
1 Pembroke Villas, Kensington, to be near the Abingdon Road works of
Bamford and Martin.

Also in May 1924 John Roby Benson joined the Bamford & Martin Company. Benson was keen to develop a new engine for the Aston Martin.

By mid-1924 Bamford & Martin Ltd. were in Lionel Martin's debt to some £31,000 and consequently his resources were stretched.

"Palings", Kingston on Thames, to which Lionel Martin and his wife moved in early 1932, and which remained their home until Lionel

Martin's death on 21st October

1945. Despite the collapse of his company in 1925, the luxuriously furnished house did not look like the home of someone in reduced circumstances.

John Benson suggested Lionel Martin approach Benson's mother Lady Charnwood and she put up £10,000 and acquired the assets of the old company. In July 1924 a new company was formed with Lionel Martin, Katherine Martin, George Eustace Ridley Shield and John Roby Benson as directors.

Among those continuing to use Aston Martins in competition were Captain Douglas at the wheel of "Razorblade" and Miss Pink who drove "AM270" at Shelsley Walsh.

On 11th November 1925, 53 Abingdon Road became the subject of having the Receiver appointed. Two days after the appointment of the Receiver (Arthur Whale), Lionel Martin found his services dispensed with and he left the works for the last time and a large part of his personal fortune lay beyond recovery.

John Roby Benson made critical remarks in the hearing of others and these got back to Lionel Martin. With having just been dismissed by the Receiver, Lionel Martin would not let such remarks go unnoticed. In fact, Lionel Martin would quickly resort to the processes of law. Benson was alleged to have said that Lionel Martin had been party with Jack Addis in removing Aston Martin working drawings without Benson's knowledge and that Lionel Martin had removed spare parts from the company at the time it was in the Receiver's hands. These were the more serious of the accusations. Lionel Martin became the plaintiff in a slander action against John Roby Benson, the defendant. Lionel Martin was represented by Sir Leslie Scott, KC. The plaintiff, Lionel Martin sued the defendant, John Roby Benson for three separate slanders alleged to have been spoken on the 18th November 1925, the 24th November 1925 and the 27th November 1925. The words complained of contained a number of serious allegations against the plaintiff and they accused the plaintiff of three felonies – larceny, criminal conspiracy and dishonesty. John Roby Benson pleaded non-publication and justification. After a trial lasting many days the jury found that the defendant had in fact published the words complained of and that as to each separate matter of justification that the plea of justification had not been proved by the defendant.

However, upon seven separate heads the jury dealt with they awarded a total of 1 ¾ d damages. Lionel Martin claimed that the Aston Martin working drawings had been removed to the company's solicitors for the benefit of anyone interested in the rescue of the company and denied being a party with Addis or anyone else in placing cast-iron bolts in the Benson engine.

But in addition to being awarded just 1 ¾ d damages, McCardie J. also refused to award Lionel Martin his costs.

"Recognizing as I do that each case must depend on its own particular facts, I am satisfied in the present action that I ought to make an order depriving the plaintiff of costs. I have no doubt that the verdict of the jury meant, either that the statements made were so nearly true that ignominious damages would suffice, or that the plaintiff's character was so bad that contemptuous damages should be given. This I think is the basic explanation of the assessment by the jury, after the fullest deliberation, of one farthing damages only upon each head of claim, including the charges of felony. Nor do I doubt that the jury took the view that in any event the conduct of the plaintiff had been open to the gravest suspicion, that it called for severe condemnation, and that the plaintiff had brought the defamation upon himself. In my opinion the jury were amply warranted, upon the circumstances revealed at the trial, in assessing the damages at the smallest sum that could be given.

I make an order depriving the plaintiff of costs.

The judgement will be entered for 1 ¾ d without costs."

Eventually, John Roby Benson's parents (the Charnwoods) purchased the goodwill and assets of the old company and approached the Birmingham firm of Renwick and Bertelli with a view to amalgamating.

On 12th October 1926 the firm of Aston Martin Motors Ltd. was incorporated and a new chapter was about to begin.

After the collapse of the company in 1925 Lionel Martin and his family continued to live at "The Hollies", Pembroke Villas, Kensington, but in 1932 they moved to "Palings", Warboys Road, Kingston-on-Thames, Surrey.

William Sommerville Renwick and Lord Charnwood owned equal parts of the new company Aston Martin Motors Ltd. Renwick had worked for Armstrong Siddeley at Coventry. It was there that he had met Augustus Cesare "Bert" Bertelli who was to design production Aston Martins of the period 1926 to 1937.

Benson and Lord Charnwood departed and in 1928 the firm was reconstructed as Aston Martin Limited. The Chairman was to be S.C. Whitehead and in 1931 Renwick left to go to America.

With the exception of the years 1929, 1930 and 1934, Aston Martin ran cars at Le Mans every year from 1928 to 1964. In 1935 Aston Martin achieved third place at Le Mans.

In 1932, Sir Arthur Munro Sutherland bought Aston Martin for his son Robert Gordon Sutherland to manage. He was to share joint managing directorship of the company with Bert Bertelli.

Bertelli and Sutherland had disagreements over what Bertelli believed was a dilution of the company's sporting pedigree. Bertelli departed from Feltham in 1937 and his assistant Claude Hill took over design.

Sir David Brown

David Brown was an apprentice who started work in 1921 at the age of 17 in a gear manufacturing works founded by his grandfather in 1860. He was not particularly keen about gears and gear-manufacturing at the beginning and would have preferred to have started off in the automobile industry, but he eventually found the art of gear-making quite fascinating and began to thoroughly enjoy work in the Huddersfield plant.

During the first year of his apprenticeship he also found time to build the inevitable "special" using a chassis of his own design and a 2-litre Sage engine. Later, when Amherst Villiers, known as a formidable tuner of motor cars, arrived in Huddersfield to ask Messrs David Brown and Sons Ltd If they would care to build a new super-charger which was to be fitted on the Raymond Mays Vauxhall Special, David Brown – now foreman in the worm-gear department – took an immediate interest in the project. At this time the David Brown Company was already making various components for motor car manufacturers.

In 1860 the David Brown organisation occupied only a small workshop and had a staff of exactly two. In 1910 the company was already considered the largest gear-making firm in the British Commonwealth and when war started in 1914, they had established a large plant in Huddersfield.

Expansion continued after the first world war and soon two old-established engineering firms, the Keighley Gear Company and P.R. Jackson Ltd. Were acquired and incorporated in the parent organisation.

It was a strange coincidence that David Brown, as foreman of the worm gear department, was responsible for the manufacture of rear axle components which were fitted in a new car designed by A.C. Bertelli and announced on the eve of the 1927 Olympia Motor Show as the Aston Martin – "the car that is built for the owner's pleasure."

David Brown and Sons built the supercharger for the Vauxhall Villiers, a car David brown later drove in circuit and sprint events. The David Brown Company also went on to manufacture superchargers for the production 4 ½ litre "blower" Bentley cars and for the Tim Birkin-Doroth Paget racing team.

In 1926 David Brown's apprenticeship ended. He was then promoted to foreman in the worm gear department at Huddersfield. In 1927 he progressed to the appointment of assistant works manager and in 1928 became manager of the Keighley gear department. In 1929 he was elected to the board of David Brown and Sons Ltd. And in 1932 became managing director at the age of 28. In later years some of his co-directors were to oppose some of his proposals and could equally have opposed his appointment as managing director at the very beginning if this had been thought necessary.

David Brown developed a new tractor of his own and it was produced in time for the Royal Show in 1939. A separate manufacturing company, David Brown Tractors Ltd. was then formed and housed in a converted cotton mill at Meltham near Huddersfield. Before the end of the Second World War, David Brown further enhanced group productive capacity by acquiring three more companies, Muir Machine Tools Ltd., David Brown Gears (London) Ltd. and the Coventry Gear Company. In 1945 he established the David Brown Tool Company.

In October 1959 at a dinner in Park Lane, London, David Brown stated that;

"I have often been asked, since winning the Sports Car Championship, 'What are your future plans?'

In answering this, I think it necessary to go back to our early days of racing, some ten years ago, when we were competing with more or less standard DB2 saloons. And to remind you just how standard these cars were, I used one of the team cars, VMF 64, for my own personal transport in between its racing appearances.

The whole character of racing has, however, changed, until today an ordinary production car would stand about as much chance in a race as the proverbial snowball of getting into hell! The sports-racing car of today has become a more complicated and expensive version of a Grand Prix car, with the addition of a self-starter, lighting, mudguards, two seats, windscreen, etc.

To remain in the hunt today it is necessary to design, build and develop completely new cars every few years.

This leads to the big question: what is the purpose of sports car racing? – and it seems to me that it has departed very much from the original intention when sports car racing first started. I would like to see sports car racing where the cars are closely allied to what the public can buy.

For Grand Prix racing, on the other hand, the problem should be of producing within a prescribed formula the fastest machine that is possible, regardless of other constraints. Both forms of racing serve a useful purpose but they should be complementary to one another and not merely variations on a theme.

I believe that sports car racing has reached an important cross-roads – and nobody appears sure which way to go. The regulations for Le Mans – only seven months away – are still unknowns and the formula laid down in 1958 for World Championships, which was to run for three years, has already, before its third year, been altered. Even the DBR1 on our stand [at the London Motor Show] is not eligible in its present form to race next year.

Furthermore, we have been racing continuously for something over ten years and during that period our production has remained fairly static. On the other hand we have developed, as a result of racing, a very fine product which seems to be very much in demand. We feel it is now time we devoted a greater part of our efforts to this commercial aspect of our business and a greater part of our technical resources to the more rapid development of our production cars.

I have strong views on what the future of sports car racing should be and it is with regret that I have to tell you that we do not intend to compete in sports car racing next year. Our own racing efforts in 1960 will be concentrated upon the Grand Prix field in this last year of the present Grand Prix Formula.

I should like to think that if, and when, we return to sports car racing, it will be something that more closely resembles our production car and what the public can buy."

David Brown visited the Feltham factory, tried the Atom saloon and bought the company with Claude Hill and Gordon Sutherland remaining.

Alan Good of Lagonda launched the LB6 in 1945 calling it the Lagonda – Bentley. A lawsuit with Rolls followed which Lagonda lost and Alan Good put Lagonda up for sale.

David Brown learnt that Rootes and Jaguar were interested in Lagonda but were deterred by the economic outlook. David Brown eventually bought the company, though not its premises, for £52,000.

Initially Aston Martin DB2/4 bodies were built by Mulliners and the Lagondas went to Tickford, Newport Pagnell. Tickford became part of the David Brown empire in 1955 and DB2/4 bodies then went there. For David Brown the best way of promoting the road cars and proving their components was to go racing. This affected much of his thinking and of those he employed.

At the same time that Aston Martin was sold to Company Developments (1972), so the tractor division was sold to Tenneco. David Brown died in 1993.

Harold Beach

Born in 1913, Harold Beach started his working life as an apprentice at the coachbuilding firm Barkers, who made Rolls-Royce bodies. After that he took a job with William Beardmore (builders of commercial vehicles) as a draughtsman at their Earlsfield factory. Then Harold Beach spent a period with another ex-Barkers employee, James Ridlington. As the war approached there was another job change for Harold Beach, this time with the Hungarian engineer Straussler at his Park Royal factory as a designer working on airfield components.

In 1950, Harold Beach saw an advert for a design draughtsman for David Brown Tractors (Engineering) Automobile Division at Feltham. After an interview with the chief draughtsman, Frank Ayto, Harold Beach started in September 1950.

Harold Beach started work on a successor to the Aston Martin DB2 at the time Eberan von Eberhorst was made chief engineer. Von Eberhorst had been with Auto-Union before the war. But Harold Beach was to find that Eberan von Eberhorst had different ideas to him and scrapped all the work they had done on a DB2 successor.

Harold Beach was involved with work on a replacement for the Aston Martin DB2/4 and this was called Project 114. But once again his plans were to be thrown into disarray. John Wyer, who had been appointed competitions manager in 1950, was made general manager in 1956. Wyer had the idea that they should go to Touring of Milan for them to style a body on Harold Beach's perimeter frame. They turned round and said they did not want to build on Beach's design but wanted a platform frame instead. Beach's front and rear suspension of Project 114 were however retained. Harold Beach's proposed perimeter frame regarded the chassis as separate from the body, while Touring of Milan's platform frame regarded the chassis and body as almost one.

The "Superleggera" principle involves a strong platform chassis and a steel framework onto which the body panels are fixed. Components such as wheel arches are thereby part of the chassis and not added afterwards gaining greater stiffness.

Harold Beach also worked closely with Tadek Marek on the redesign of the 2.9 litre engine.

The Aston Martin DBS was introduced in 1967 and Harold Beach was responsible for its chassis and suspension. And it featured a de Dion rear axle that Harold Beach had proposed on a production model ten years earlier.

In 1972, David Brown, who had owned Aston Martin since Harold Beach joined them 22 years previously, sold the company to a property company called Company Developments. They decided to keep Harold Beach on.

In 1973 the chairman, William Willson, made Harold Beach director of engineering.

From June 1975, Harold Beach continued to work with the new owners Peter Sprague and George Minden, though no longer as a director.

Harold Beach retired in 1978, having served under three ownerships.

Tadek Marek

Tadek Marek was born in Krakow, Poland in 1908. He graduated from Charlottenburg Technical Institute in Berlin with a diploma in engineering.

After the war Tadek and his wife Peggy went to Germany for a short period but returned again to Britain.

In 1948 he got a job with the Austin Motor Corporation at Longbridge.

He left Austin and despite a job offer with Holden Motors in Australia, went to Aston Martin. It was probably Feltham general manager James Stirling who was responsible for bringing Tadek Marek to Aston Martin.

The 1950's saw many significant Aston Martin characters coming and going. In 1950, Harold Beach, John Wyer and Robert Eberan von Eberhorst joined the development team. Others who joined included stylist Frank Feeley, chief draughtsman Frank Ayto and designer Willy Watson.

Among those who left Aston Martin were Gordon Sutherland, Jock St. John Horsfall and Claude Hill.

When Tadek Marek had finished his apprenticeship under Harold Beach he made improvements to the old 2.9 engine which was a temporary measure until the introduction of an all-new unit.

The "new" 2.9 litre engine was first seen in the DB Mark III that was introduced in March 1957 and although the cubic capacity remained the same it had a new block, new crankcase and new oil pump.

Tadek's redesign of the 2.9 engine showed his talent for this sort of work and gave Aston Martin breathing space until work could begin on an all-new engine for the all-new Aston Martin DB4.

What shortcomings that remained in Tadek Marek's 3.7 litre engine for the Aston Martin DB4 were finally put right in the 4.0 litre engine that was fitted to the Aston Martin DB5 in July 1963.

In the early 1960's John Wyer decided work should commence on a new engine to power the next generation of Aston Martins and concluded a V8 configuration would be best. Tadek began work on designing this engine in 1963. As it came from the drawing board the unit was a 4.8 litre capable of developing 324 bhp with four vertical twin choke carburettors.

Tadek Marek did all the engine design drawings himself and he had a man in the design department working for him called Alan Crouch who did all the design and layout work.

Victor Gauntlett

Born in 1942, Victor Gauntlett made much of his money from the petrochemicals industry.

In 1980, Victor Gauntlett put £500,000 into Aston Martin Lagonda which amounted to a ten per cent stake. In 1981 he became executive chairman at a time when Aston Martin were producing four cars a week. It was Victor Gauntlett who, in the 1980's, renewed the association with Zagato and Aston Martin sold fifty-two Vantage Zagato coupes which cost £86,000 each.

Prior to coming to Aston Martin he had founded and sold Pace Petroleum and in 1988 he founded Proteus Petroleum. He died in 2003, aged 60

Alan Curtis

Alan Curtis had been interested in Aston Martin in 1975 and had been prepared to pay £650,000 for the company. But he learned it had been bought by a consortium comprising Peter Sprague (an American) and George Minden (a Canadian). But the Englishman of the consortium was no longer involved and Peter Sprague called Alan Curtis saying he had heard that he was interested in saving the company and that without an Englishman he (Peter Sprague) would not continue.

So in 1975, Aston Martin Lagonda's quartet of shareholders were Peter Sprague, George Minden, Alan Curtis and a retired steel businessman Denis Flather.

At the end of 1975, Alan Curtis along with Denis Flather became directors of Aston Martin. In March 1977, Alan Curtis became managing director of Aston Martin.

Four members of the senior management were made associate directors and these were Mike Loasby (director of engineering), David Flink (director of manufacturing), Nigel Butten (director of finance) and Tony Nugent (director of sales).

Rex Woodgate

Rex Woodgate was born in 1926 and had a job as an equipment tester at British Acoustic Films. Then he got a job with Thomson and Taylor who built racing and record breaking cars at Brooklands. He worked as a mechanic to Stirling Moss, preparing his car for the 1949 season, before joining H.W. Motors of Walton-on-Thames as a mechanic until 1950. Reg Parnell recommended Rex Woodgate to John Wyer and he was engaged to build production versions of the Aston Martin DB3S in 1954.

Rex Woodgate also worked on the DB3S's replacement the DBR1 and then the DBR2.

In the middle of 1961, Rex Woodgate rejoined Aston Martin and was factory service representative for North America. Rex Woodgate was convinced that Aston Martin should set up its own importership rather than using several importers and distributors. In May 1964, Aston Martin Lagonda Incorporated was opened near Philadelphia and it stayed there for fourteen years.

In 1971, Rex Woodgate was made President of Aston Martin Lagonda Incorporated.

Ted Cutting

In 1949 he was working for Sydney Allard but applied for a nearby job at Feltham with Aston Martin. His work was to be a new chassis frame for the Aston Martin DB2. After the 1955 Le Mans he was made Chief Racecar Designer and worked on the Aston Martin DBR1. He used a multi-tubular spaceframe design but Aston Martin had problems with the David Brown CG537 gearbox that was used on the DBR1.

Ted Cutting was also involved with the DP212, DP214 and DP215 project cars of Aston Martin DB4 front suspension and steering gear. Ted Cutting remained with Aston Martin until 1964.

William Towns

In 1936 William Towns was born, fairly near to Guildford. In 1955 William Towns joined the Rootes Company and found that there was a department within the Rootes Company that did in full size what he had done as a lad with plasticine. The person in charge of Rootes' styling studio at the time was Ted White. Ted White as the department Head of Styling was more an administrator than stylist because management (seven members of the Rootes family) were the stylists and the supposed stylists were more akin to modellers for the management.

William Towns stayed with Rootes for eight years before moving to Rover for more money and at a time the Rover 2000 was being developed. William Lyons, upon seeing the full-scale wooden mock-up of the Rover 2000, thought that its styling was abysmal and that it was badly proportioned. But Towns thought that the interior was excellent.

While at Rover, William Towns worked on three projects. The first involved working on proposals for a Targa-topped two plus two sports car based on the Rover 2000 saloon. Sketches were made but nothing came of them. William Towns next project concerned the gas turbine racer that was developed for Le Mans. For the 1963 Le Mans the gas turbine racer was entered as an open roadster. But for the 1965 Le Mans, William Towns was to develop a closed body version of the gas turbine racer. Towns produced a scale model which was subsequently wind tunnel tested before being made into a full-size body. The third project was a car intended for the film world. William Towns drew up a very low sports, based again on the Rover 2000 platform. Although a quarter-scale model was made nothing came of it once again.

William Towns had been at Rover three years when somebody mentioned that there was a job going at Aston Martin. But Aston Martin did not have a styling job on offer; they had openings for a body engineer and for a seat designer. William Towns went to them and they offered him a job designing seats at first.

Later, Harold Beach told William Towns they wanted to do a four door car. Towns explained that you have to design the four door version first and then shorten it if you wish to make a two door. William Towns was later asked to produce scale models of his proposals and he created a two door and a four door side by side. The latter became the Lagonda model of 1974.

In 1969 William Towns was offered the job of Chief Stylist at Triumph but he preferred to work for them on a freelance basis. Replacements for the Triumph 1300 and 2000 saloons (code-named Puma and Bobcat) were cars that Towns was brought in to work on.

Aston Martin kept in touch with William Towns and when the 6-cylinder Aston Martin DBS became the V8 he produced the styling. However, proposals for gull-winged versions of an Aston Martin and Lagonda came to nothing.

Augustus Bertelli

Many regard Augustus Bertelli as the father of Aston Martin. Bertelli was born in the Italian town of Genoa in 1890; he and his family moved to Cardiff in 1894. On leaving school he took up a general engineering apprenticeship in Cardiff. He then, took a job with Fiat in Turin. Bertelli was riding mechanic to Felice Nazzaro in a Fiat for the Coppa Florio. Grahame-Whites, manufacturers of French aircraft, took Bertelli on to develop an engine of his.

Augustus Cesare Bertelli married Vera in 1918 at Hendon, and they moved to Golders Green. Bertelli was given a job at Birmingham-based Alldays and Onions and he designed a new Enfield-Alldays car.

In 1924, Bertelli and W.S. Renwick teamed up in business in Birmingham. Renwick and Bertelli bought Aston Martin from John Benson and kept him on. Really, John Benson had nothing but the goodwill of Aston Martin. Augustus Bertelli and W.S. Renwick then moved to Feltham and they then took on Claude Hill. Within a year of starting at Feltham, they had produced a completely new Aston Martin with a 1 ½ litre engine. The end of the 1920s and the start of the 1930s saw the Aston Martin name carried on the 1 ½ litre series and had names such as International, Ulster and Le Mans.

Augustus Bertelli's brother, Enrico Bertelli, ran a coach-building business next to the Aston Martin factory at Feltham, hence the beautiful bodies of the early Aston Martin cars in an era of genuine hand-built cars.

Benson and Renwick eventually left the company and Claude Hill left twice, once in 1928 and once in 1934. In 1936, Bertelli left and the company was in the control of the Sutherland family at a time when the 2-litre cars were being introduced.

Just before World War II, Bertelli took a job with a firm called High Duty Alloys, where he stayed until 1955.

Richard Stewart Williams

Richard Williams has been involved with Aston Martin all his life, having begun an apprenticeship with Aston Martin in 1962 while they were still at Feltham and just before the move to Newport Pagnell. Here he gained valuable experience in the engine department.

In the mid-1960s he left the company to run Sellers Racing, a team created by motoring enthusiast, former Goon and film star Peter Sellers. Richard Williams was responsible for the road cars of Peter Sellers that were based in Geneva. This came to an end in 1968 and he set up in business as R.S. Williams Ltd. in a railway arch in Brixton's Coldharbour Lane.

By 1971, Richard Williams had many influential clients. Richard Williams came to prepare Project 212 for historic racing; the Project 212 car was owned by Viscount Downe (President of the Aston Martin Owners Club) and driven by Mike Salmon. In 1982, Aston Martin specialist Robin Hamilton's Group C Nimrod Project came into being. Downe bought one, and under Richard Williams experienced direction, was driven to 7th place at Le Mans by Salmon and Mallock.

Later the Ecurie Ecosse C2 team that Richard Williams was managing succeeded in winning the 1986 World Championship. Richard Williams became Managing Director of Proteus Technology. The season of 1989 proved to be successful as the AMR1 finished in every race in which it was entered, including 4th place in the World Sports Prototype Championship round at Brands Hatch.

Richard Stewart Williams now runs a business, Richard Stewart Williams Ltd, which operates from Protech House in Cobham, Surrey; they are the only people to have built complete cars for Aston Martin, the Sanction 2 Zagatos. These cars sold for the highest price ever achieved for a new Aston Martin, thanks to Victor Gauntlett and his sales skills. They were sold for half the price of an Aston Martin DB4GT Zagato, which at the time was £1.5million, so the Sanction 2 cars sold for £750,000. Richard Stewart Williams has also developed the 6.3 litre and 7 litre V8 engine conversions, and the 4.2 and 4.7 six-cylinder engines.

John Wyer

Born in Kidderminster in 1909, John Wyer took a five-year apprenticeship with Sunbeam when he left school and then moved to Solex Carburettors in 1934. After the war he became an unofficial Bugatti agent and did some hill climbs in their 3.3 litre models. In 1947 John Wyer took a job with Monaco Engineering, one of England's most well-known race-preparation companies.

In 1950 John Wyer was approached by industrialist David Brown who offered him a post as racing manager. Initially intended as temporary, John Wyer was with Aston Martin for 13 years. He nearly resigned in 1950 when David Brown indicated he wanted to drive one of his own cars at Le Mans in 1950. He was spared that decision when the RAC Competitions department declined to approve David Brown's participation.

In 1956 David Brown offered John Wyer the post of General Manager of Aston Martin Lagonda. Reg Parnell, now retired from driving took over team management duties.

John Wyer still played a significant part in road-car and racing planning through to 1962 when Aston Martin withdrew from competition. In 1952 John Wyer had spent three weeks in hospital with burns when Reg Parnell's 3-litre Aston Martin caught fire during a refuelling stop at Goodwood.

A highlight in John Wyer's years at Aston Martin was 1959 when Carroll Shelby and Roy Salvadori took the Aston Martin DBR1 to victory at Le Mans. Aston Martin also went on to win that year's World Sports Car Championship.

In 1962 John Wyer and David Brown had a major policy disagreement. David Brown wanted to produce a Lagonda saloon which was effectively going to be a stretched four-door Aston Martin DB4. John Wyer believed it would not be commercially viable and he was proved correct. At the end of June 1963, John Wyer left Aston Martin after 13 years.

Following talks with Ford, John Wyer became European Resident Manager, Special

John Wyer, Daytona, 1972.

Vehicles Activity. He became a key member of Ford's multi-million dollar assault at Le Mans. He established Ford Advanced Vehicles, becoming General Manager, operating from Slough. Ford Advanced Vehicles became responsible for about 100 GT40's over the next three years, and Wyer was involved with getting Ford's first victory at Le Mans in 1966.

On 1 January 1967, Ford Advanced Vehicles became JW Automotive, Wyer's own company. In 1968 a JW Automotive GT40 won Le Mans when driven by Pedro Rodriguez and Lucien Bianchi. From 1970-1971 JW Automotive entered into a Partnership with Porsche.

In 1972 Gulf Research Racing was established in the old JW premises in Slough with

John Wyer at 1000km Spa 70

President Grady Davies. John Wyer was a non-executive director.

On 8th April 1989, John Wyer died in Scottsdale, Arizona.

Ian Callum

Ian Callum was the man behind the shape of the Aston Martin DB7. The Scot studied Industrial Design at Glasgow School of Art and contributed to projects such as the Ford RS200 Group B rally car. In 1990 he set up TWR's design studio and was working on a Jaguar-based sports car – a project that eventually led to the production of the Aston Martin DB7 in 1993.

Eric Thompson

Eric Thompson was born on 4th November 1919 at Dutton Hill near Surbiton in Surrey. He was a stockbroker who worked for Lloyds of London, the historic shipping company.

His first race came in September 1948 in the 'Douze Heures de Paris', Montlhery. He finished 4th in the one-and-a-half litre class and 17th overall. He competed in many national events in his own HRG.

In 1950 Eric joined Aston Martin and along with Dennis Poore and Pat Griffiths were to support a trio of Aston Martin professional drivers. They were Peter Collins, Reg Parnell and Roy Salvadori. In a Connaught A-Type (Chassis A6), Eric Thompson had his one and only World Championship Grand Prix appearance at the British Grand Prix at Silverstone over the weekend of 17-19th July 1952 and gained ninth place. The event was dominated by the works Ferraris of Giuseppe Farina, Alberto Ascari and Piero Taruffi.

At the Goodwood 9 hrs of 1953, Eric Thompson and Reg Parnell drove an Aston Martin DB3S to victory. In 1955 Eric Thompson retired from top line driving but not before tackling Le Mans and finishing 16th at the Goodwood 9 hrs of that year.

Arthur Wilson

Arthur Wilson began working for Aston Martin in the engine build shop early in 1959, when the Aston Martin DB Mark III and DB4 were in production.

In the 1970s he worked for David Morgan, who was Chief Engineer on engines at that time.

In 1984, Aston Martin Tickford and Aston Martin Lagonda separated and AML did not have an engineering department. Michael Bowler was given the job of setting up a new department at Newport Pagnell for AML and Arthur Wilson was offered a job in charge of engine development.

Arthur Wilson retired from his position as V8 Powertrain Engineering Manager and Chief Engineer at Aston Martin in September 2000 after 41 years of service.

Bob Dover

Bob Dover was born in Essex in 1945 and gained a First Class Honours Degree in Mechanical Engineering from Manchester University. He started as a Facilities Engineer with British Motor Holdings and later joined Massey Ferguson in Coventry. He was Manufacturing Director in charge of manufacturing and quality at Jaguar in 1987 and 1988.

Bob Dover was appointed Managing Director and Chief Executive Officer of Aston Martin in January 1997 and became Chairman in April 1997. Under his stewardship, Aston Martin Lagonda launched the Aston Martin V8 Volante, Aston Martin DB7 Vantage, Project Vantage and V8 Vantage Le Mans. He also instigated the Aston Martin Vanquish programme and played a significant part in the acquisition of the Gaydon factory.

David Richards

On 11th March 2007, Aston Martin Lagonda was sold to a consortium headed by Prodrive founder David Richards. Ford retains a £40 million investment in Aston Martin Lagonda whilst Kuwait-based companies Investment Dar and Adeem Investment hold the majority shareholding, with David Richards and American banker John Sinders having the remainder.

David Richards Banbury-based Prodrive developed the GT1 Class Aston Martin DBR9 and GT3 DBRS9 racers for Aston Martin and co-formed Aston Martin Racing to run works entries in the FIA GT Championship.

David Richards established his first business, David Richards Autosport Ltd, in the mid-1970s but pursued a career in rallying and eventually won the 1981 World Rally Championship as Ari Vatanen's co-driver.

Mike Loasby

Mike Loasby started his career at Alvis Cars and when Rover took over Alvis in 1965 he became senior designer of engines at Coventry Climax.

He went to Aston Martin as Development Engineer in 1967. After joining Triumph Motor company he returned to Aston Martin in 1974 to become Chief Engineer.

In 1978 Mike Loasby joined the De Lorean Motor Company and after that he formed his own company Midland Design Partnership.

In 1989 he was recalled to Aston Martin to work as a consultant on the Aston Martin Virage and Lagonda saloons and shooting brakes.

Walter Hayes

A printer's son, Hayes went into journalism and quickly rose through the ranks to become editor of the Sunday Dispatch newspaper at the age of thirty-two. There he employed no less an authority than Lotus boss Colin Chapman to write a "different" motoring column, beginning an association that would yield greater things by the end of the 1960s.

In 1962 Hayes moved to Ford as Director of Public Affairs, where his remit included motor sport. Hayes convinced Ford to invest £100,000 in a new 3-litre Grand Prix engine to be designed by Keith Duckworth at Cosworth – Duckworth's first complete engine design – and used in Chapman's Lotuses. Hayes also persuaded Chapman to hire a "star" second driver in the shape of Graham Hill, alongside established Lotus number one Jim Clark. The DFV famously won its debut race in the back of Clark's Lotus 49, and it went on to become the most successful Formula 1 engine ever made, with over 150 wins to its credit.

Hayes also helped to broker a deal between Carroll Shelby and AC Cars. He was involved with Ford Advanced Vehicles, the Slough-based subsidiary that built GT40s, and championed the formation of the Advanced Vehicle Operation at Aveley where the first "RS" Escorts were built. Later, Hayes would persuade unwilling production-line chiefs to build specialized Escorts among more run-of-the-mill machines, keeping Ford at the top of international rallying.

Hayes rose to the level of vice chairman of Ford of Europe before his retirement in 1989. Even in retirement he remained close to Henry Ford II, and was behind the company's investment in AC and later Aston Martin. Hayes was persuaded out of retirement to run Aston Martin, where he kick-started the project that would create the DB7 and ensured it reached production, along the way cementing ties between the modern Aston Martin and David Brown, whom he described as the company's "patron saint".

Hayes retired, again, in 1994. He died at the age of seventy-six in December 2000.

Henniker Mews where Aston Martin started out.

The building in Henniker Mews where Aston Martin started in 1913 is now marked with this plaque marking 100 years

Next to 53 Abingdon Road is Vantage Place; few of the locals realise its significance

Inside Vantage Place today

On the wall of Vantage Place is this sign showing it was formerly the works of the makers of Aston Martin

Its current premises are on both sides of the road in Tickford Street.

Aston Martin Works, Newport Pagnell

Above can be seen Aston Martin's showroom in Newport Pagnell and below the Aston Martin Heritage Centre next to it.

Aston Martin Vantage Race Car

The Aston Martin Vantage race car seen here at Silverstone

Aston Martin Vantage Race Car

Aston Martin Vantage race car seen here in Newport Pagnell

Aston Martin V8 Vantage

The Vantage is the third car, after the Vanquish and the DB9, to use Aston's VH platform – a chassis of lightweight aluminium extrusions, pressings and castings bonded and riveted together in a process similar to that used in the Lotus Elise. Previously these chassis were built by an outside contractor, but now they are constructed in-house at the spectacular new Gaydon factory in Warwickshire.

The chassis contributes only 183 kg to the Aston's kerbweight of 1590 kg. The V8 Vantage is 50mm shorter and 40mm lower than a Porsche 911 Carrera S, and considerably more compact than the DB9; 313mm shorter, 60mm lower and with a 140mm shorter wheelbase.

Moving from front to back, the familiar Aston grille spreads out into a wide-arched front with pronounced wheelarches, before flowing tightly back into a typically compact coupe form. It then bulges back out with thick-set rear arches and a cut-off tail under which nestle fat twin tailpipes.

The engine is at the front, but is mounted considerably back in the chassis, with drive passing to the rear wheels via a carbonfibre propshaft surrounded by a cast aluminium torque tube. The six-speed manual gearbox is at the rear along with the limited-slip differential, aiding the excellent weight distribution of 51:49 front to rear.

The new V8 engine's capacity has been increased from 4.2 to 4.3 litres and now features dry-sump lubrication to better withstand cornering forces and allow it to be fitted lower in the chassis. With a unique bore and stroke, the Aston V8 has its own pistons, conrods and crankshaft, along with its own head, manifolds and each of the 32 valves. There's variable timing on the inlet camshaft, plus a resonance induction system, and the spent gasses are expelled through a 4-2-1 manifold on each bank of cylinders and out of an exhaust system that features a bypass valve to boost noise above 4,500 rpm.

Acceleration In Gear					
mph	2nd	3rd	4th	5th	6th
20-40	2.5	3.6	4.9	7.5	7.7
30-50	2.3	3.3	4.5	7.3	7.3
40-60	2.2	3.1	4.3	7.2	6.9
50-70	2.3	3.0	4.1	7.0	6.5
60-80		3.1	4.0	6.7	6.2
70-90		3.2	4.1	6.8	6.2
80-100		3.4	4.4	6.9	6.3
90-110			4.8	6.9	6.4
100-120			5.6	7.4	6.9
110-130				7.9	
120-140				8.7	
130-150				10.3	

The results of all this are 380 bhp at 7,300 rpm and 302 lb ft of torque at 5,000 rpm. Stopping this are 355mm discs at the front and 330mm discs at the rear.

Once started, the engine gives an old-fashioned V9 sound where you can almost hear each piston stroke. The exhaust keeps the flaps open from idle to around 2,000 rpm, so moving away and loping along is accompanied by an industrial muscle-car gurgle.

One of the main strengths of this car is its easy-going nature around town and in traffic. The ride quality sets the Vantage apart from its rivals, as it soaks up surface changes and irregularities with genuine talent.

Despite this apparent cosseting, the Vantage is nevertheless a car that you have to really drive. The gearlever moves around the gate with a sturdy mechanical feel that often requires effort from the shoulder. Both the brakes and the clutch require confident application and the steering has a weighted feeling as the wheel turns in your hands.

Aston's claim of 4.9 seconds for the 0-60 mph sprint is correct, trailing the Carrera S by three tenths of a second and

Engine	
Type/ Fuel	V8, 4300cc/petrol
Made Of/ Installation	Alloy/front, longitudinal, rwd
Power/ Torque to Weight	242bhp/ 192lb ft per tonne
Specific Output	88bhp per litre
Comp Ratio/ Bore/Stroke	11.3:1, 89.0/86.0mm
Valve Gear	4 per cyl, DOHC per bank

the 500bhp BMW M6 by two. By 100mph, attained in 11.5 seconds, the gap to the 911 has widened to seven tenths and the M6 (9.7 seconds) is rather rapidly disappearing up the road.

Stopping the V8 from such great speeds is no great drama as the grooved discs prove more than up to the task. The initial hard-pedal resistance is similar to the db9's brakes, but unlike that car's vague modulation, the Vantage's stoppers can really be leant on with reassurance once you are used to them.

The Vantage is a forgiving and sympathetic car to drive. It grips well when required, and slips into understeer as the limit approaches before adopting a tail-out stance. At this point, a stab of throttle will keep the car sliding in a progressive and entertaining manner, although you will need a fair few revs on the dial if you are to have accurate control of the slide. If the road surface is slippery, it will readily oversteer with the DSC off, but as our wet circuit experience proved, when driven in such a manner, it's easier to control than a 911.

Chassis and Body	
Construction	Bonded aluminium structure
Weight	1570kg
Drag Coefficient	0.34
Wheels	Alloy (f) 8.5Jx19, (r) 9.5Jx19
Tyres	235/45 ZR19, 275/40 ZR19 Bridgestone Potenza
Spare	Mousse

Dimensions	
Front Track	1568mm
Rear Track	1562mm
Width including mirrors	2022mm
Width excluding mirrors	1866mm
Front Interior Width	1385mm

Suspension	
Front	Double wishbones, coil springs, anti-roll bar
Rear	Double wishbones, coil springs, anti-roll bar

Steering	
Type	Hydraulically-assisted rack and pinion
Turns lock-to-lock	3.1
Turning Circle	11.1m

Brakes	
Front	355mm ventilated discs
Rear	330mm ventilated discs
Anti-lock	Standard, with EBD
Parking brake	Hand operated

Aston Martin V8 Vantage

Known at Aston Martin as AM305, the Vantage was presented in concept form at the North American International Auto Show in 2003, and in production form at the 2005 Geneva Show. The car was shaped by Aston Martin design director Henrik Fisker.

Aston Martin V8 Vantage

Aston Martin Vantage uses a 4.3 litre engine

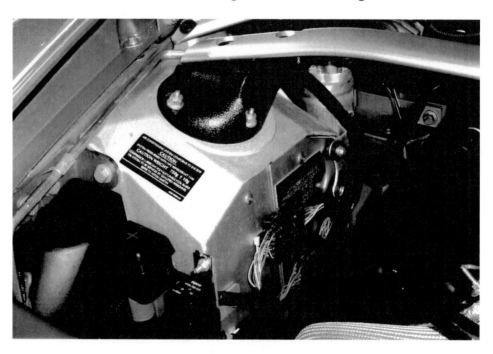

Aston Martin V8 Vantage

Engine bay of the Aston Martin Vantage

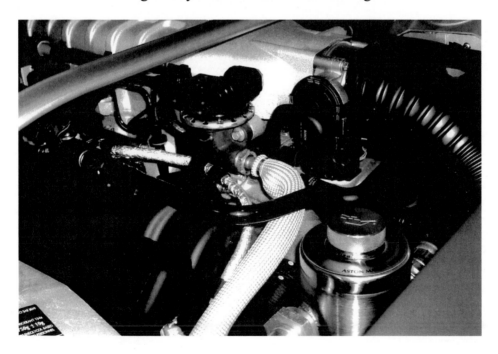

Aston Martin V8 Vantage

Interior controls of the Aston Martin Vantage

Aston Martin V8 Vantage

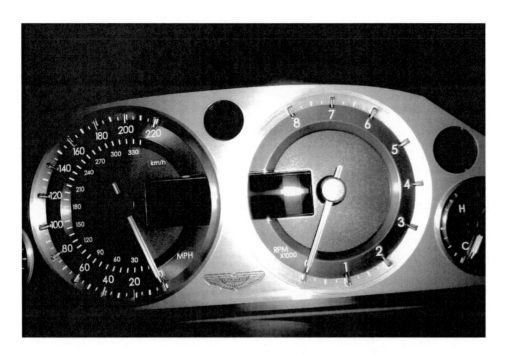

Speedometer of the Aston Martin Vantage

Aston Martin V8 Vantage

High quality leather steering wheel of the Aston Martin Vantage

Metal plaque showing that the Aston Martin V8 Vantage is hand-built

Aston Martin V8 Vantage

Door trim of the Aston Martin Vantage

The 4.3 litre Vantage is a strict two-seater

Aston Martin V8 Vantage

Air vent and interior controls of the 4.3 litre Vantage

Aston Martin V8 Vantage

Below, the Prodrive Rally GT Vantage

Aston Martin Vantage

Aston Martin Vantage is seen here in Knightsbridge, London.

Aston Martin Vantage

The Aston Martin Vantage has the distinctive number plate 2 JKC

Aston Martin Vantage Convertible

A convertible Aston Martin Vantage is seen here at the Sheraton Hotel, Knightsbridge

Aston Martin Vantage Convertible

The convertible Aston Martin Vantage is available in the UK from June 2007.

Aston Martin Vantage N24

Specifications	
Cost	£92,500
Engine	4280 cc, V8
Maximum Power	410 bhp @ 7300 rpm
Maximum Torque	313 lb ft @ 5000 rpm
Specific Output	96 bhp per litre
Power to Weight	308 bhp per tonne
Weight	1330 kg
Length	4380 mm
Width	1865 mm
Height	1255 mm

Aston Martin Vantage N24

This pair of Aston Martin Vantage N24s were seen at Silverstone.

These two cars, one number 4 and the other 42, are both left hand drive.

Above can be seen the engine bay of the Vantage N24, whilst below an interior shot of the N24 badge. The car is built by Special Vehicle Operations.

Aston Martin Vantage N24

The Aston Martin Vantage N24 Racer seen here on the track at Silverstone.

Aston Martin DBR9

Specifications	
Cost	£558,000
Engine	5935 cc, V12. Twin chain-driven overhead camshafts per bank and four valves per cylinder. Visteon twin PTEC engine management, and fuel injection. Pectel engine ECU.
Power	600 bhp @ 7000 rpm
Weight	1100 kg
Length	4687 mm
Width	1978 mm
Height	1195 mm

Aston Martin DBR9

The Aston Martin DBR9 Engine

The engine team at Aston Martin Racing and led by Jason Hill developed a version of the Aston Martin DB9 V12 that has a full 6.0 litre displacement.

Breathing through two 31.2 millimetre air intake restrictors it produced about 585 bhp which is a competitive figure for GT1. The penalty of cutting to a pair of 30.8 millimetre restrictors would put output down to about 570 bhp. Also running an air conditioning compressor off of the nose of the crankshaft will sap power and how much power is lost depends on temperature.

For cars running with air-conditioning the maximum allowable cockpit temperature is 32 degrees centigrade.

Engine of the Aston Martin DBR9.

Aston Martin DBR9

This is measured by the ACO (Automobile Club de l'Ouest) with a sensor in the vicinity of the driver. The ACO do allow cars to run without air-conditioning but the cockpit temperature must not be 12 degrees above ambient. Additionally, if cockpit temperature goes above 32 degrees centigrade the car must be fitted with additional homologated driver cooling devices.

Running with air-conditioning brings with it an 0.3 millimetre increase in the relevant restrictor size. The Aston Martin DBR9's V12 engine sends considerable heat back towards the cockpit as the car's aluminium shell is not as good a thermal barrier as cars that use the more common steel production. With a front engine car more heat goes into the cockpit than a mid-engine car.

Aston Martin Racing is run out or Prodrive's Headquarters at Banbury. They also operate Subaru's World Rally Championship programme. Prodrive have been commissioned to run Aston Martin's racing programme since 2005 and this will be for a period of at least five years. The Aston Martin GT1 project sees co-ordination and co-operation from Prodrive at Banbury and the manufacturer which has its headquarters at Gaydon, some thirteen miles away.

Aston Martin DBR9

At Gaydon, Warwickshire, former Le Mans prototype designer Graham Humphries oversees technical liaison, while at Banbury, Oxfordshire, the GT1 project is overseen by AMR Technical Director George Howard-Chappell, engine development being headed by Jason Hill. The GT1 Le Mans programme is a part of Aston Martin Racing, but so is producing customer GT1 and GT3 cars.

Opening or closing louvers in the top of each front wheel arch is another way of altering downforce.

Aston Martin DBR9

The Aston Martin DBR9's monocoque shell starts out as a set of aluminium extrusions made by Hydro Aluminium Extrusions. Racing modification work is done by AMR. Then they are assembled at the Hydro Plant in Worcester around the tubular steel roll cage that has been manufactured at Banbury.

The Aston Martin DBR9 monocoque structure goes into the bonding oven with the cage already in place, ensuring the best possible integration between sheel and cage.

Aston Martin DBR9

The cockpit of the Aston Martin DBR9.

Aston Martin DBR9 Racing Record

Unless stated, all races were in the GT1 class

Date	Event	Drivers	Car No.	Laps	Result
2005	Sebring 12hrs	David Brabham Darren Turner Stephane Ortelli	57	338	4th place
2005	Sebring 12 hrs	Peter Kox Pedro Lamy Stephane Sarrazin	58	303	15th place
1st Oct 2005	Petit Le Mans	David Brabham Darren Turner Jonny Cane	57	378	4th place
1st Oct 2005	Petit Le Mans	Pedro Lamy Thomas Enge Peter Kox	58	359	11th place
15th Oct 2005	Laguna Seca	Peter Kox Pedro Lamy	58	156	9th place
15th Oct 2005	Laguna Seca	Darren Turner David Brabham	57	155	10th place
2006	FIA GT Oschersleben	Deletraz Piccini (Phoenix Racing)	5	125	3rd place
2006	FIA GT Oschersleben	Gollin Babini (Aston Martin Racing BMS)	23	125	5th place
2006	FIA GT Oschersleben	Pescatori Ramos (Aston Martin Racing BMS)	24	124	6th place
2006	FIA GT Oschersleben	Wendlinger Peter (Race Alliance Motorsport)	33	124	7th place
2006	FIA GT Spa	Lemeret Deletraz Piccini (Phoenix Racing)	5	589	2nd place

Aston Martin DBR9 Racing Record

2006	FIA GT Spa	Pescatori Babini Enge (Aston Martin Racing BMS)	23	578	4th place
2006	FIA GT Spa	Wendlinger Peter Bouchut (Race Alliance Motorsport)	33	413	29th place
2006	FIA GT Paul Ricard	Wendlinger Peter (Race Alliance Motorsport)	33	87	4th place
2006	FIA GT Paul Ricard	Gollin Babini (Aston Martin Racing BMS)	23	86	5th place
2006	FIA GT Paul Ricard	Deletraz Piccini (Phoenix Racing)	5	86	6th place
2006	FIA GT Paul Ricard	Pescatori Ramos Malucelli (Aston Martin Racing BMS)	24	79	16th place
2006	FIA GT Dijon	Peter Wendlinger (Race Alliance Motorsport)	33	132	2nd place
2006	FIA GT Dijon	Piccini Deletraz (Phoenix Racing)	5	132	3rd place
2006	FIA GT Dijon	Babini Pescatori (Aston Martin Racing BMS)	23	132	6th place
2006	FIA GT Dijon	Gollin Ramos (Aston Martin Racing BMS)	24	131	7th place

Aston Martin DBR9 Racing Record

2006	FIA GT Mugello	Wendlinger Peter (Race Alliance Motorsport)	33	86	1st place
2006	FIA GT Mugello	Babini Pescatori (Aston Martin Racing BMS)	23	86	5th place
2006	FIA GT Mugello	Piccini Deletraz (Phoenix Racing)	5	86	6th place
2006	FIA GT Mugello	Gollin Ramos (Aston Martin Racing BMS)	24	4	Did not finish
2006	FIA GT Budapest	Babini Malucelli (Aston Martin Racing BMS)	23	102	3rd place
2006	FIA GT Budapest	Piccini Deletraz (Phoenix Racing)	5	102	4th place
2006	FIA GT Budapest	Gollin Ramos (Aston Martin Racing BMS)	24	102	6th place
2006	FIA GT Budapest	Peter Wendlinger (Race Alliance Motorsport)	33	63	Did not finish
2006	FIA GT Adria	Babini Pescatori (Aston Martin Racing BMS)	23	144	4th place
2006	FIA GT Adria	Gollin Ramos (Aston Martin Racing BMS)	24	143	5th place

Aston Martin DBR9 Racing Record

2006	FIA GT Adria	Wendlinger Peter (Race Alliance Motorsport)	33	61	Did not finish
2006	FIA GT Adria	Piccini Deletraz (Phoenix Racing)	5	35	Did not finish
2007	FFSA GT Nogaro Race 1	Bornhauser Mackowiecki (Larbre Competition)	3	37:58.905	30th place
2007	FFSA GT Nogaro Race 2	Bornhauser Mackowiecki (Larbre Competition)	3	1:01:32.958	5th place
2007	FFSA GT Ledenon Race 1	Bornhauser Mackowiecki (Larbre Competition)	3	25:47.177	26th place
2007	FFSA GT Ledenon Race 2	Bornhauser Mackowiecki (Larbre Competition)	3	55:31.371	4th place
2007	FFSA GT Dijon Race 1	Bornhauser Mackowiecki (Larbre Competition)	3	1:01:31.319	6th place
2007	FFSA GT Dijon Race 2	Bornhauser Mackowiecki (Larbre Competition)	3	1:01:24.101	3rd place
2007	FFSA GT Val de Vienne Race 1	Bornhauser Mackowiecki (Larbre Competition)	3	1:02:04.447	2nd place
2007	FFSA GT Val de Vienne Race 2	Bornhauser Mackowiecki (Larbre Competition)	3	1:01:58.571	3rd place
2007	FIA GT Zhuhai	F. Babini J. Davies (AMR BMS)	23	69	4th place
2007	FIA GT Zhuhai	J. Kane J. Cocker (Barwell Motorsport)	17	68	8th place
2007	FIA GT Zhuzai	K. Wendlinger R. Sharp (Jet Alliance Racing)	33	68	9th place

Aston Martin DBR9 Racing Record

2007	FIA GT Zhuzai	G. Mondini F. Monfardini (AMS BMS)	22	68	11th place
2007	FIA GT Zhuzai	R. Lechner L. Lichtner-Hoyer (Jet Alliance Racing)	36	66	15th place
2007	FIA GT Silverstone	K. Wendlinger R. Sharp (Jet Alliance Racing)	33	66	4th place
2007	FIA GT Silverstone	J. Davies F. Babini (Aston Martin BMS)	23	65	7th place
2007	FIA GT Silverstone	J. Cocker Johnson (Barwell Motorsport)	17	65	10th place
2007	FIA GT Silverstone	R. Lechner L. Lichtner-Hoyer (Jet Alliance Racing)	36	64	11th place
2007	FIA GT Silverstone	Toccacelo Monfardini	22	64	12th place
2007	FIA GT Bucharest	K. Wendlinger R. Sharp (Jet Alliance Racing)	33	72	4th place
2007	FIA GT Bucharest	J. Davies F. Babini (AMR BMS)	23	69	9th place
2007	FIA GT Bucharest	R. Lechner L. Lichtner-Hoyer (Jet Alliance Racing)	36	10	Did not finish
2007	FIA GT Bucharest	Toccacelo Monfardini	22	24	Did not finish
2007	FIA GT Monza	K. Wendlinger R. Sharp (Jet Alliance Racing)	33	66	1st place
2007	FIA GT Monza	F. Babini J. Davies (AMR BMS)	23	66	6th place
2007	FIA GT Monza	R. Lechner L. Lichtner-Hoyer (Jet Alliance Racing)	36	66	7th place

Aston Martin DBR9 Racing Record

2007	FIA GT Monza	Monfardini Toccacelo (AMR BMS)	22	64	12th place
2007	FIA GT Oschersleben	J. Davies F. Babini (AMR BMS)	23	80	3rd place
2007	FIA GT Oschersleben	Alessi Monfardini (AMR BMS)	22	78	6th place
2007	FIA GT Oschersleben	K. Wendlinger R. Sharp (Jet Alliance Racing)	33	40	Did not finish
2007	FIA GT Oschersleben	R. Lechner L. Lichtner-Hoyer (Jet Alliance Racing)	36	1	Did not finish
2007	FIA GT Spa-Francorchamps	F. Babini J. Davies F. Monfardini (AMR BMS)	23	330	Did not finish
2007	FIA GT Spa-Francorchamps	K. Wendlinger R. Sharp L. Lichtner-Hoyer R. Lechner (Jet Alliance Racing)	33	158	Did not finish
2007	FIA GT Spa-Francorchamps	Toccacelo Frassinetti Lancieri (AMR BMS)	22	13	Did not finish
2007	Le Mans 24 hrs	Brabham Turner Rydell (Aston Martin Racing)	009	342	5th place
2007	Le Mans 24 hrs	Bouchet Gollin Elgaard (Aston Martin Racing Larbre)	008	340	7th place

Aston Martin DBR9 Racing Record

2007	Le Mans 24 hrs	Herbert Kox Enge (Aston Martin Racing)	007	337	9th place
2007	Le Mans 24 hrs	Babini Davies Malucelli (Aston Martin Racing BMS)	100	336	11th place
2007	Le Mans 24 hrs	Garcia Menten Fittipaldi	59	318	17th place

Aston Martin DBR9 Teams

Aston Martin Racing

David Brabham
Tomas Enge
Johnny Herbert
Peter Kox
Rickard Rydell
Darren Turner

Aston Martin Racing BMS

Giorgio Mondini
Ferdinando Monfardini
Fabio Babini
Jamie Davies

Jet Alliance

Ryan Sharp
Robert Lechner
Lukas Lichtner-Hoyer
Karl Wendlinger

Barwell Motorsport

Johnny Kane
Jonny Cocker

Larbre Competition

Gregor Fisken
Cristophe Bouchut
Greg Fanchi
Gabriele Gardel
Fabrizio Gollin
Steve Zacchia

Team Modena

Christian Fittipaldi
Antonio Garcia
Gene Lee
Jos Menten

Aston Martin DBR9

Front views of the Aston Martin DBR9.

Aston Martin DBR9

The Aston Martin DBR9 has OZ Racing forged magnesium 19 inch wheels and uses Michelin 235/40 ZR 19 tyres at the front and Michelin 275/35 ZR 19 tyres at the rear.

Aston Martin V8 Vantage S

The Aston Martin Vantage S Convertible seen here in Knightsbridge, London

Aston Martin V8 Vantage S

Above, can be seen the driving position in the
Aston Martin Vantage S Convertible

Aston Martin V8 Vantage S Specifications	
Engine:	V8, 4735cc, petrol
Power:	430bhp @ 7300 rpm
Torque:	361 lb ft @ 5000 rpm
Power to Weight:	267 bhp per tonne
Specific Output:	91 bhp per litre
Compression Ratio:	11.0 to 1
0 - 62 mph:	4.5 seconds

Aston Martin V8 Vantage S

Aston Martin V8 Vantage S Dimensions	
Length:	4385 millimetres
Width:	1865 millimetres
Height:	1260 millimetres
Wheelbase:	2600 millimetres
Fuel Tank:	80 litres
Boot:	80 litres

Aston Martin V8 Vantage S Specifications	
Front Suspension:	Double Wishbones, coil springs, anti-roll bar
Rear Suspension:	Double wishbones, coil springs, anti-roll
Brakes:	380 mm ventilated discs (front) 330 mm ventilated discs (rear)
Wheels:	8.5J x 19 inches (front) 10J x 19 inches (rear)

Aston Martin V8 Vantage S

Centre console of the Aston Martin V8 Vantage S

Front leather seats of the Aston Martin V8 Vantage S

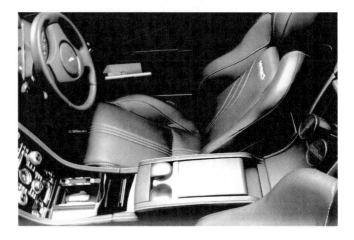

Another view of the driving position in the Aston Martin V8 Vantage S

Aston Martin V12 Vantage S

The AM28 engine increases peak power to 565bhp

The AM28 5.9 V12 replaces the 5.9 litre V12 engine of the Aston Martin DBS

Aston Martin V12 Vantage S

The V12 Vantage S does 0 -
62mph in 3.9 seconds

V12 Vantage S badge can be seen
on the rear of the car